PREFACE

I watched my three children become curious about what to study in high school. They began seeking opinions from their peers and from respected adults. As I tried, sometimes without much luck, to advise them about classes, which college they should attend (obviously they were teenagers and already knew everything), and the careers they should consider, I started jotting down my thoughts about the beginnings of my own business career and the mistakes I made and continue to make. As I expanded on these thoughts, they turned into this book. I hope it will help you with your own career decisions.

A few people that edited this text told me that sometimes I write with the tone of a big brother and at other times as if I am annoyed. The parts where I seem to be annoyed involve chapters and issues where I see the potential damage to the readers that are just coming into the workforce. I pull no punches because I don't want you sidetracked even by a well-intentioned person. We know there are many well-intentioned people who are clue-less. I am always dismayed at who people turn to for advice. Just because someone is successful in business doesn't mean that he or she has a clue about how to raise kids or how to save a marriage.

We will first talk about how and whom to get advice from, and then cover what "successful" might mean to you. We will then look at how to get the best from your education before looking at the traits you have, how to work on your goals, and how to triangulate your relationships to get a job. You will also read about how and why to net-work, do things that unsuccessful people won't, and other thoughts about business and life.

I will not bore you with statistics that corrobo-rate my views or findings. (You will learn that you can always find statistics that will support anything if you look hard enough.) My lessons come from real-life experiences during thirty years in the pro-fessional business world. I have had the opportuni-ty to work for an accounting firm, small and large real estate firms, and on Wall Street. I have been able to move from the local business level to work on national and international stages.

Oh, by the way, any semblance between the characters in this book and real-life people, living

CAREERS:
BE SAVVY,
BE TRUE TO YOURSELF
AND
DON'T BE A
MORON

Turn work into a hobby

JACK MINTER

ISBN: 1461095891
ISBN-13: 9781461095897
Library of Congress Control Number: 2011906114

or dead, is merely coincidental, unless the story is about you.

I did not write this book for those who are trying to stay in college as long as possible or for those who whine about not being successful or that a supervisor is "keeping me down" for some ridiculous reason. I wrote it for people who want to achieve and continue to move forward with their careers.

I trust this will help you on your journey as you work through academia and begin your walk through your business life.

TABLE OF CONTENTS

The best advice is this: Don't take advice and don't give advice. ~Unknown

It is a good divine that follows his own instructions. ~William Shakespeare

Old men are fond of giving good advice, to console themselves for being no longer in a position to give bad examples. ~François La Rochefoucauld

When we ask advice we are usually looking for an accomplice. ~Charles Varlet de La Grange, *Pensées*, 1872

We hate to have some people give us advice because we know how badly they need it themselves. ~Unknown

CHAPTER 1—
OPINIONS OR ADVICE?

As the old saying goes, "Opinions are like butts, everyone has one."

On one hand, it is great to be inquisitive enough to ask people what they do for a living and how they got where they are. On the other hand, you need to be able to filter through their opinions and be able to apply that information to your personality and skills. We probably all think we do this, but most of us don't.

We usually have a difficult time judging ourselves properly. Most of us try to hold ourselves responsible for our own actions, but we seldom do. We all try to analyze our skills and determine a course of action based on the current job market. We may be working on a degree, working to improve our situation in a current career, or even looking outside our current career toward a different goal. It seems at some point many people become stumped or lost in this endeavor and begin to ask for advice from others that they feel can help them. A real problem can develop when you ask for opinions from people who are not qualified to advise you. If you trust these people, you may assume that their opinions equate to good advice.

Another situation that occurs while analyzing your options is that you can ask too many people for their opinions or advice and end up getting many different answers, which could confuse you and slow down the process.

And like butts, everybody has one!

Types of advice

I run into two types of advice and opinions. The first is the one where you ask for the opinion or advice, or someone is interested or critical enough to offer you this service for free without your asking.

The second is a little more difficult to see and more difficult to manage. This type shows itself through pressure and manipulation. How I see this type is a parent or other family member pressuring or advising someone on what to do with his or her life or career. Take, for example, when I was leaving college to go home.

The day after I graduated from college, I packed my small pile of earthly possessions that were worth driving from Texas to Wyoming with and just before leaving called home to tell the parents I was on my way home. Luckily for me—didn't seem that way when it happened—Dad picked up the phone. I told him I was headed home and would be there the following day. This started him going through a list of things to do around the house, the ranch, and at work that he seemed to have put off for me to do for quite some time. As he continued the list, I started really thinking what it would be like to live and work around that type of pressure from him to do what he wanted, not what I wanted. I had just finished getting my accounting degree, was dating my future wife, and really didn't want to go back to Wyoming at that time.

After getting off the phone, I sat in the truck thirty minutes or so thinking of what I wanted to do versus what he had told me I had to do. I decided I wasn't going to go home. I picked up the phone again and told Mom and Dad my decision to stay and make my own way.

Sometimes, well-meaning people, usually family members, push to have you join their profession, one they worked in before they retired or the "family" business. This can work out well if that is your choice too. It seems we all have a tendency to want people to do what we do. An example is people who are getting married or are married. They seem to want everyone to be engaged or married. Same thing when they are having kids, buying a house, or going on vacation. It seems to help them justify their decisions. You should listen but make your own decisions for your reasons. Hopefully they will respect that.

My parents didn't like my decision and laid the guilt trip game on me for a while. Sometimes that works and sometimes it doesn't. Whether it does or not, taking or giving advice in this manner usually causes hard feelings because it's a way to manipulate and control people. Don't let people do this to you and don't do it to others. Be careful of letting it happen with people who pay you, people you are dating, parents, spouses, etc. Don't let others control you, and don't manipulate or try to control others.

Taking advice

Now you may not like to hear what I will be saying here since you will have to assume control and responsibility for your life. This will include all of your successes and failures that will occur over the years. As you will finally realize, life is all about decisions. The better decisions that you make and put into practice, the better your chances of achieving your definition of success. Broad economic issues like meltdowns in the markets make even great decisions difficult to pay off at times. I have watched people who have determined their decisions, then disciplined their lives, come out of economic downturns better off than those who do not. This course allows them to achieve their goals more quickly.

Dealing with opinions or advice is a slippery slope. This may not seem to be a huge issue, and you may not have received some terrible advice that changed your life for the worse, but if you have, you will understand and agree.

The only way to get through this minefield called a career is to have your own sense of success and the profession that may get you there. Since "success" is such a broad subject, it will need to be discussed in the following chapter. You have to do your own homework and not rely on others. This is extremely difficult to do and it will force you to look inwardly and make decisions on your own, for yourself. You won't be able to blame anyone else if you make decisions based on your own findings and ideas. This may be why people let others help them too much or make decisions for them. If they aren't successful, it "isn't their fault."

Giving advice

As you become successful, an interesting phe-nomenon will occur; people will ask for your ad-vice about areas in which you do not have any experience. I am good at my profession, and I al-ways strive to be the best I possibly can. However, that certainly does not make me any kind of ex-pert on other topics such as marriage, raising kids, doing laundry, gardening, etc. I find it fascinating that people ask me about all of these issues.

Most people who achieve success—as they de-fine it—can't help giving out opinions or advice. If given properly about a subject, by someone who really is an expert, it can really help. Sadly, after a spate of success, many people think they are all-knowing about all subjects. These people can really mess up naïve people's lives. Before you do this, help them find someone who has achieved the professional success that they are aiming for. As long as this person is not a moron (see later chapters for more information on morons), he or she would be the right person to give advice.

We need to take charge of ourselves and seek out the correct people to help us because we now realize that most people will give opinions and advice even if they don't know what they are talking about. I am asking each of you to help stop the madness of unqualified people giving advice. If you know these facts then you can only blame yourself for your misfires during your career. However, most of us would rather do the easy thing: blame someone else.

TAKEAWAYS: You will need help in your life and professional career, but beware. People often give unwanted or unmerited advice if you ask the wrong people or sometimes just because they think they should. Also watch out for the familial or financial pressure that pushes or pulls you into situations or jobs that are not the ones you planned on. Take control of your own life and career! You may want to establish what I have heard called a "board of advisers" for your life. Each board member will have expertise in areas that apply to your life.

Success isn't a result of spontaneous combustion. You must set yourself on fire. ~Arnold H. Glasow

If you want to make your dreams come true, the first thing you have to do is wake up. ~J. M. Power

Try not to become a man of success, but rather try to become a man of value. ~Albert Einstein

Eighty percent of success is showing up. ~Woody Allen

Success consists of going from failure to failure without loss of enthusiasm. ~Winston Churchill

Success is more permanent when you achieve it without destroying your principles. ~Walter Cronkite

Always bear in mind that your own resolution to success is more important than any other one thing. ~Abraham Lincoln

I didn't feel I was really successful until I owned forty hunting dogs. ~T. Boone Pickens

CHAPTER 2—SUCCESS

What does "success" mean to you? People have very different definitions of success, and definitions will change throughout our lives. Some think that success is a healthy balance between family and career. Others are more focused on material goals such as a certain title or a particular net worth. This is a very personal topic that you will need to address for yourself.

I grew up near a small town in Wyoming on a farm and ranch, and my grandparents were cotton farmers in West Texas. I thought I would be successful by becoming a farmer or rancher or, better yet, a veterinarian with a farm and ranch. Based on my experience, I could make a lot of money doing what I thought I would like to do. Seems reasonable, right?

By talking with the local veterinarian, I learned that I would need to study diligently to become a veterinarian. That was the first time I remember a decision that I had made turn into an action. I had heard I needed good grades to become a veterinarian and with that goal in mind, I began focusing on getting the grades I needed. Weird what a goal can do for you!

I graduated from high school, and my grades were good enough to get me into a college known for helping students qualify for veterinarian school. I started with a pre-veterinarian curriculum. My goal as I studied was to get into a good veterinarian school. I followed this program for two years before I decided to intern with a veterinarian and see what the profession was like. The only veterinary practice I had seen was the "country vet" who mostly took care of farm and ranch animals with some time spent on dogs, cats, birds, and other small critters that were around the area. I usually saw our veterinarian only when he came out to take care of some of our cattle or horses.

As I started working with the veterinarian that summer, I quickly realized that he was on call 24/7 with all types of animals. People seemed to have no issue calling him day or night with any kind of problem their livestock or pet had.

I may have romanticized veterinarians because of the work they do, the extra money they seemed to have, and from reading *All Creatures Great and Small* by James Herriot. He wrote several delightful books about his experiences as a country veterinarian in rural England. He had funny stories about his practice that made the life seem great. However, I never realized that when he was called out of a warm bed on a cold, wet night in the middle of winter to "pull a calf" (help the momma cow give birth), it was only funny after the fact. I can tell you that it isn't pleasant pulling a calf in the middle of a Wyoming blizzard at three in the morning! I have a friend who has lost three wedding rings doing this because his hands got so cold and numb.

After some experiences with the veterinarian, and seeing that many of his clients couldn't pay for his services, I started thinking of other career paths. The lesson I learned from this is that you really have to enjoy what you do for a living. Even making a lot of money, when you aren't enjoying your work, is not what life is about! You will not be good at what you are trying to do if you don't enjoy it.

When the summer ended, I headed back to college to look into other degree choices. Because my plan to be a veterinarian had gone by the wayside, I didn't know what I should study. I knew that I didn't want to spend many years at school—I couldn't afford it and didn't love studying all of the time.

During my internship, I noticed that although the veterinarian was great at his work, he always complained about the business side of his practice. I helped him work on his books, and while the bookkeeping wasn't that enjoyable, I was able to get his financial statements ready to send to his accountant for his review and tax preparation.

After some thought and study about a degree, I decided to major in accounting. Like many things we do, I enjoyed some of the studies but not others. Thankfully, I graduated and got a job at a small firm that mostly did tax accounting, and I really enjoyed the work. I could help people with their tax issues, which allowed me to do some research and have the human interaction of meeting with the clients. I had found something that I was good at and enjoyed!

After a few years at this firm, I got my CPA license. I ended up working at Arthur Andersen in the tax department for a few years and then met my next employer, a real estate firm. I had found the career that I was best suited for and had learned to focus on the goal of being the best I could be at that career. If you continue working at each job and focus on being the best, it will either become your career or it will enable you to move into a different job because of your expertise. Without being good at what I was doing, the clients I had would have never asked me to leave and work with them.

As I mentioned, my definition of success has changed throughout my life and career. I remember doing many things as a young man that weren't very wise because I was trying to impress someone of the opposite sex. Back then, I was successful if I talked a girl into going on a date with me. Like a popular country song says, "The Chicks Dig It!"

Once out of college, I landed the job that I wanted. I had worked diligently in school and wanted to achieve the success that I had envisioned. The next step in my quest for success was to accumulate money and possessions. I thought of the saying, "You work your fanny off to make money to buy things to impress people you don't even like!"

Today, analyzing what success means for me has become easier. Many of the things I thought would make me look or be successful I have either achieved or found that they did not fit my definition of success. I have figured out that success grows or breeds upon itself. In most instances, success can be related to your goals. New successes or goals can be added or taken away once you have achieved that success or goal or decided that it was not right for you.

I have learned one very important thing about success. Once you have achieved a success that you set for yourself, celebrate and revel in your success! Enjoy that moment, and then re-evaluate your definition of success. Consider defining your next success and setting your goals to achieve it.

My current definition of success in business is this: I continue to add great team members to an already dominant team of professional real estate sales professionals. For me, I am success-ful when building dominant teams that service cli-ents as effectively and efficiently as possible, using "bleeding edge" technology.

I used to guide folks to achieve what I thought would mean success for them, but I have found that this task is difficult if not impossible. I no longer do that and give advice only if asked, if I feel it won't be wasted, and if I feel I am truly the correct coach for the person.

TAKEAWAY: Define what success means to you, but know that this will change through-out your life and career. When your situa-tion changes, and it will, don't be afraid to reevaluate your definition.

No man who worships education has got the best out of education...Without a gentle contempt for education no man's education is complete.
~G. K. Chesterton

The aim of education should be to teach us rather how to think, than what to think—rather to improve our minds, so as to enable us to think for ourselves, than to load the memory with thoughts of other men.
~Bill Beattie

An educational system isn't worth a great deal if it teaches young people how to make a living but doesn't teach them how to make a life. ~UnknownIt is a thousand times better to have common sense without education than to have education without common sense.
~Robert G. Ingersol

The object of education is to prepare the young to educate themselves throughout their lives.
~Robert Maynard Hutchins

CHAPTER 3—EDUCATION, "THE YELLOW BRICK ROAD"

Let's talk about the "yellow brick road" of education.

I assumed that the reason to go to college was to acquire the skills needed in order to obtain that first job. That's why I went! I have been told that I am a "dinosaur" in this respect. Today people tell me that you don't go to school just to find that first job. You are supposed to have a "unique collegiate experience" by traveling and studying abroad. While that may be a great direction for a student who is contemplating an overseas position or is studying a language, it doesn't make a lot of sense for others. Because this "unique collegiate experience" is expensive, you can only assume that either there is a rich uncle writing checks or the college has made travel part of a scholarship program.

For students who have to pay for their own education, the burden of debt for their "unique collegiate experience" means paying off student loans for many years. I'm not sure that, with the costs of college today, the cost/benefit of a college education can be justified. You may sense some animosity in this chapter. I have had three children in private schools this past year. The cost of this was like driving a very expensive SUV off a cliff every semester. Thank goodness two have graduated. I prefer not to go into an analysis of the cost/benefit of the cost of a college education. However, I do know that while my children were at school, several of their classmates had to leave the private school and go to state or community colleges to finish their degrees. Even then they will be so burdened with debt that they cannot begin to enjoy life.

To make it worse, many people find that the degree they spent so much money for is not going to help them enter the career they want to pursue. What a pity! You need to know what you want to study early on. Some students make career decisions and take classes that they later find were a waste of time. Usually these students have not prepared properly by getting advice from the correct people or interning with a firm that is in the industry they think will be the best fit for them.

Most colleges and universities have programs that will help you with this. My kids thought highly of their schools' career centers. They will help you understand how to prepare for an interview, what classes certain industries require, help with getting internships, and many other things. I know my kids used them to help develop their resumes, and they took personality and aptitude tests there. All of these services are expensive once you are out of school. You should take these tests early in your college career to help you ascertain what you are good at.

This is not to say overseas travel is a waste of time. I have traveled extensively and there is nothing that will expand your horizons any faster or better. You *should* see the world. But do it after you graduate. There is no point in spending a semester in Italy if you are going to take the same classes you would take back home. Travel on your own time—it's much cheaper!

The son of one of my colleagues did very well in high school and was accepted at a prestigious college. He enrolled and started his "unique collegiate experience." Unbeknownst to his family, he was concerned about the cost of college since he could not decide what career he wanted to go into. He felt he was wasting his time and his money going to school without a goal in mind. During his first year, he talked with his parents about dropping out of college to enter the armed forces for a few years until he had an idea of what he wanted to do. They agreed. He is currently a navy officer, has narrowed his career choices, and feels that he will now be able to take full advantage of his college experience, and get it paid for!

It is refreshing to hear of someone taking control of his own destiny.

To decide on the type of education that is best for you, talk with someone who is in the position you are working toward or someone who hires people into that position. Ask that person what programs you should pursue, not what a counselor or recruiter who hasn't worked in that industry recommends.

It is tough to get into college. With the large numbers of American students and increasing numbers of foreign students, it is difficult to get into the university you want unless you understand the requirements of that college and put the right amount of effort in. The same issue will arise four (or five) years down the road when these students graduate; the competition for jobs will be tough. If you want a specific position, prepare yourself for it now to give yourself the best advantage.

This may seem like a daunting task. You may wonder how to contact the right people, how to figure out what classes you should take, or what type of internships you should pursue. Start with your family. If you know someone through your family connections who can advise you, that's great. If not, you will have to do some research and probably move outside your comfort zone to discuss these questions with the correct person.

Almost every industry has a professional organization. Contact it. The organizers want to help you. They will have contacts that can mentor you and help you to better understand their profession.

With the help of the Internet and other research tools, you can find individuals who are spokespersons for the industry you are researching. Contact them. (Do you notice a pattern evolving?) They will be happy to carve out some time to help you, but be thoughtful about their time. They are very busy people and will not have time to chat. But, they will have time for a short thoughtful conversation with them that will be extremely valuable to you.

Be aware that some "mentors" have large egos and like to "help" people understand the path they took to be the "raging success" they are today. Let them tell you all about themselves. They think they are very special and may feel that they had no help achieving what they have in their profession. You may need to reference the moron chapter to properly deal with this person. Do not let this deter you from calling others.

These suggestions will help you consider if a certain career path is right for you and what you can do to successfully enter that profession.

Additionally, I have met too many people who never consider two critical factors of certain careers: how much money you can earn and how much time you need to spend at work.

Some folks are pushed into careers by a parent, a friend, or a spouse.

I have a friend who decided to be a teacher while he was in college. Both of his parents had been educators, and so he decided on the same path. I have family members who have been and still are teachers, and it is truly one of the most admirable professions. Sadly, teachers do not make a lot of money, and my friend soon realized this. That shouldn't have been much of a shock. Teachers aren't included on Forbes' "Top 100 Richest Americans" list. Find out what the average pay is for the profession you are contemplating and the financial steps to take as your career progresses. The amount of pay in certain jobs should not be a surprise.

Some of the traditionally highly paid professions like medicine and law require a tremendous amount of time, commitment, and sacrifice. Know what it takes to get to the highest levels in one of these professions before committing to a career—these professions burn through people who haven't counted the costs. They all require long hours, extensive and expensive schooling, and continuing education. If you don't have a passion for this type of work, this isn't a career for you.

TAKEAWAY: Finding the right career path is a difficult journey. There are many distractions (like international study), and you might start in a career only to find that it is not the correct path for you. It will take continuous effort, and you will have to tread outside your comfort zone. Do your research. Make phone calls. Contact as many of the *correct* people as you can.

No matter where you go, there you are.
~Confucius

A man is ever apt to contemplate himself
out of all proportion to his surroundings.
~Christina G. Rossetti

What we do flows from who we are.
~Paul Vitale

We do not deal much in facts when we are
contemplating ourselves.
~Mark Twain

How many legs does a dog have if you
call the tail a leg? Four. Calling a tail a leg
doesn't make it a leg.
~Abraham Lincoln

What was once called the objective world
is a sort of Rorschach ink blot, into which
each culture, each system of science and
religion, each type of personality, reads a
meaning only remotely derived from the
shape and color of the blot itself.
~Lewis Mumford, "Orientation to Life," *The
Conduct of Life*, 1951

CHAPTER 4—DON'T RACE COWS

It is amazing to watch people try to do a job that goes completely against their nature. You have fabulous salespeople who end up in management because they are so good at sales. You see managers decide to move into sales when they couldn't sell a heater to an Eskimo! Does that make any sense? No! They end up hating their new role, or the people who report to them end up hating them. Tragically, this situation usually ends one of two ways: the new manager quits and returns to sales or, worse, stays in management until he destroys the company.

I have found throughout my career that it is possible to enhance your skills by additional schooling or on-the-job training. I have also found that I cannot change someone's personality no matter how much schooling or training he receives. Certain careers are easier and more fulfilling for people who have certain personalities. I'm not saying that you might not be successful in a position that doesn't completely fit your personality, but you will probably be happier and more content if you find the career that fits.

Growing up, I spent a lot of time with animals. I'm not sure that many readers will appreciate the analogies I am about to make, but they will illustrate the point I am making.

To create a proper barnyard, you need every kind of farm animal. You have the chickens, ducks, cows, sheep, goats, and the horse. You will also need to have different breeds of a few of the animals. One example is the cow. Some cows are bred to be milked, while others are fattened up and slaughtered for meat. Another example is the horse. Some are bred to pull wagons, and some are bred to win the Kentucky Derby.

These animals cannot change what they were born to do. However, with different training or care, you may be able to increase the speed or stamina of the race horse, and with the correct feed and habitat, increase the amount of milk the milk cow gives. I hope you see where I am headed here; I won't belabor the point.

It continues to amaze me when a "milk cow" comes into my office and feels slighted because no one wants to let him run around the track. You obviously have someone who looks in the mirror and sees the reflection of a horse when actually a milk cow is looking back. This individual is going to be a terrible "racing milk cow" and because he has delusions about his skills, he will also make a terrible milk cow.

If you are a horse, be a great horse. If you are a cow, be a great cow!

Many people want to be some kind of superstar. Whether you hop around playing an air guitar or daydream of sinking a long putt to win the Masters, you can have outrageous fantasies. A lot of you still do. Most of us finally give up these dreams and work at a career that allows us to pay our bills.

Let's use a sport analogy. I know so many wannabe athletes who think they truly have the goods to be great. It is so disheartening when these folks finally realize that they do not have the talent or correct physical shape to compete at the level they always dreamed of. Even though they cannot achieve the goal they desired, they at least learned to discipline themselves in their quest to achieve their goal.

The other side of the equation—which to me is not just disheartening but pathetic—is the individual who is the physical shape and has the God-given talent to be truly great but who lacks the necessary discipline or temperament to achieve a goal. You hear coaches describe these athletes as "uncoachable." I once heard it put like this: "There is a lot of give up in that boy." You often hear these folks complain about not being understood or blaming others for unfairly taking their position on the team.

Who does not enjoy watching the athletes who have the desire and the talent to achieve their goals? They show us that with talent and focused desire, you can accomplish amazing things. When one of these athletes achieves goals, whether in golf, basketball, or any sport, you hear about it around the office for days.

We have the same problem in the business world. There are a great number of people in business who see themselves achieving greatness. Like the folks who dance around playing the air guitar or dream about the long putt, they see themselves running an organization, starting and leading a successful company, or being the greatest salesperson. As in the sports world, many people can play at a certain level, but only a few have both the talent and the desire to play at the highest levels. Like any superstar, to play consistently at that level, you have to both have the skills, the discipline and the heart.

Understand who and what you are

Never be content with your skills! Superstars continue to practice and work with coaches to improve the skills that need the most help.

In the business world, I see people who want to step up to do additional tasks, which, if they aren't ready for those tasks, will merely create more issues or slow down the process. It seems that these individuals will learn a skill, but before they use that skill to help the organization or train others, they are trying to learn another new skill.

Here is an example. When my kids were young, they were always trying to "help" me with the yard work. They particularly wanted to help me mow the yard. One would put a foot on each of my feet and then reach up as high as he could and hang onto the handle. We would get to walk very slowly with little steps around the yard. Obviously, this greatly extended the time it took to mow the yard, because each kid would have to "help."

Once the kids got old enough to actually mow the yard, I couldn't get them to do it anymore.

It isn't an issue of not wanting or not helping people to continue their growth and learn new skills. The issue is delivering those skills for a time so that there is a payback for the people who taught you and the organization that spent the time and money training you. Assume that you will then teach those who come into the organization after you.

An example of this in business is that most industries have specific software they use to analyze different metrics. If you are going to be in that industry, you will need to learn and understand that software so you will be able to move to the next level at the firm. Usually a class will teach the basics and the terminology and then you will get help from either a more experienced peer or your superior that has mastered the software and now can teach you the best way to use it for the issues you will be dealing with. You will need to show that not only have you mastered the software but also have the ability to train when you have others working with and for you. When you start teaching, remember that you just learned and you shouldn't be a smartass about your amazing knowledge to them. Heck, you just learned these skills yourself!

This seems to be a lesson that many people never learn.

TAKEAWAY: You can't change your personality, so don't try. Make the most of your personality by focusing and enhancing your skills. You will need to discipline yourself to achieve your goals.

Obstacles are those frightful things you see
when you take your eyes off your goal.
~Henry Ford

When a man does not know what harbor
he is making for, no wind is the right wind.
~Seneca

Goals are dreams with deadlines.
~Diana Scharf Hunt

Though no one can go back and make
a brand new start, anyone can start from
now and make a brand new ending.
~Unknown

It is never too late to be who you might
have been.
~George Eliot

CHAPTER 5—BIG HAIRY-ASS GOALS (AND SMALLER ONES TOO)

One of my friends is a successful real estate executive. He introduced me to an unusual phrase that I continually use.

At an annual meeting, just after a merger with a similar company, he addressed our group. He described how each company had been successful and how we could easily surpass the goals that each group had made. One of the main reasons for the merger was to cut costs and increase production for the combined entity.

He showed everyone a slide that had the abbreviation BHAG on it. The slide included several bullet points stating that the merger would double the revenue of the individual companies. I had no idea what BHAG meant and stupidly sat there with the other people who didn't want to embarrass themselves by asking about BHAG. Finally, curiosity got the better of me, and I had to ask. He acted a bit smug and announced that BHAG meant "Big Hairy-Ass Goal."

This man regularly writes down his goals. Then, during the annual review of his partners and staff, he requires them to do the same. He knows that having these goals helps his team focus on similar business goals, and he knows that he stands a much better chance of achieving the goals if people write them down. When he sees a great opportunity, he posts a BHAG for everyone to focus on.

I don't think I have ever met a successful person who didn't have written goals. There are successful folks that do not have written goals, but I would challenge them that if they did write down their goals, they could be even more successful. I have read a multitude of books on this subject and really don't have one that I recommend over others. The best thing you can do is to write down your goals and as you start using them, read books about goal setting and use those strategies to focus on your specifics. Better than that, sit down with a pen and paper and write down your goals. Many things in life need to be done rather than just read about. This is one of them!

Come up with your own BHAGs. Divide your goals into categories such as business, personal, and spiritual. A friend of mine runs a considerable portion of a large public company, runs in Ironman decathlons, has a great family life, and balances his life much better than most. He selects five business goals each year, writes them down and has the list laminated, and takes them with him wherever he goes. On the top center of his desk, in front of his calendar, he has his five goals for each area of his life with additional comments so he won't be sidetracked.

Another professional I know writes his goals on a bathroom mirror at his house so that every morning, he is reminded of what he is working toward. I have spoken to many people who write their goals down, and they tell me they usually achieve or surpass their goals if they write them down. These people often have mentors who write down goals and keep them available to review.

There is no doubt in my mind if you write down and focus on your goals, you cannot help but be successful. If you then take your business goals, write them down with your team, and focus on them, I again predict that you and your team cannot help but be successful. It is extremely powerful to have everyone in your group striving for the same business goals and executing them.

Let's make this even more usable for you. Decide what you want to do or achieve and figure out the steps or "mini-goals" that will get you there. Let's say that you have decided you want to work at a real estate firm as an analyst. You are taking finance courses at a good college and have good grades. What should your next steps be?

Research the firms you want to work with and see what they require in terms of grades and other things. Find out who their recruitment officer is (if it a smaller firm, find out who hires new analysts from school), and see if you can get a meeting with him or her. Use the Internet to find out who the officers are, if you know any of them or know someone who knows them. It is easier to get a meeting with someone who is an acquaintance.

Once you have found someone you would like to work with, find out what other skills you would need. In some cases, there are industry-specific software programs to learn. In the real estate sector, we use one called Argus, a cash-flow modeling tool that most real estate investment companies use to value their properties. You can take classes to learn Argus so that you can go to work immediately once a company hires you.

Focus on getting an internship during the school year or during the summer. An internship will help you understand what you are getting yourself into; there is a big difference between studying about a profession and doing it! Another benefit of an internship is that it will enhance your resume. In a difficult employment environment, you will need every advantage to get the job you desire.

By planning and thoughtfully deciding which steps need to be done and in what order, you can achieve this difficult task. For a certain position, most candidates work diligently at finding relationships that will help them get the internship or interview they want. Having a personal referral to interview with someone for a job or an internship is extremely helpful. You must also make sure you have all of the technical abilities that the job requires. Even then, you may not get the position you want. Make sure that you give yourself some options (a different firm to work with, a different area of the firm, another position with the same firm, or a firm in another location).

Don't get frustrated and down on yourself through this process; it is difficult. Be patient and learn from each situation so you will be able to improve. Going through this process teaches you many things, the most important being your determination.

Now I know I promised in the preface not to bore you or lie to you using statistics; however, this chapter is critical enough that I will add statistics here. People who diligently write and keep written goals are 1,000 percent more successful than people who don't. Ya think you should do this?

TAKEAWAY: Write down your goals here (if not here, write them somewhere) and follow through on them!

_____

_____

_____

_____

_____

_____

_____

_____

_____

_____

_____

_____

_____
_____
_____
_____
_____
_____
_____
_____
_____
_____
_____
_____
_____
_____
_____
_____
_____
_____
_____
_____
_____
_____
_____
_____
_____
_____
_____
_____

Some of the world's greatest feats were accomplished by people not smart enough to know they were impossible.
~Doug Larson

All morons hate it when you call them a moron.
~J. D. Salinger, *The Catcher in the Rye*

It's not who you are that holds you back, it's who you think you're not.
~Unknown

It ain't what they call you, it's what you answer to.
~W. C. Fields

Whether you think you can or think you can't—you are right.
~Henry Ford

If you hear a voice within you say "you cannot paint," then by all means paint, and that voice will be silenced.
~Vincent Van Gogh

All good is hard. All evil is easy. Dying, losing, cheating, and mediocrity is easy. Stay away from easy.
~Scott Alexander

CHAPTER 6—MORONITY AND MEDIOCRITY

If you are unlucky enough to start your career working for a moron, you may never recover! On the other hand, if you begin your career with a strong, growing, achieving company and manager, your career will likely kick off nicely.

This chapter is difficult. You see, if you aren't a moron you will read this and be bobbing your head yes the whole time. However, if you are a moron, you won't get it. If you are only turning into a moron you will get it and bob your head every now and then and then hopefully, save yourself. As we noted in the chapter about racing cows, many folks look into the mirror with preconceived notions of who they are versus what they see looking back. It will be difficult for them to view themselves as the moron they may be. This chapter will help you to decide if they or (possibly you) have any of these tendencies.

Generally, well-run organizations with non-moronic managers are looking for people with a strong desire to help build and grow an organization. The companies and managers are always looking to hire great people, not just people that they can boss around. Non-morons hire strong candidates, and because they are not morons, they hire strong candidates who will push them to fulfill their goals and expectations for themselves and their firm.

Many companies are filled with morons who never really achieve any level of success. These morons generally hire morons because they are insecure, concerned they will be found out, and afraid that they will be passed over for a promotion or higher pay. They are usually saved from being fired or passed over because they have moronic managers protecting them.

If you are hiring people, it is difficult to screen for the "moron trait." I asked a few human resource professionals if they could set up tests to determine if someone was a moron. I even asked if you could just come right out and ask candidates if they are morons. Of course, they couldn't, but they did raise their eyebrows a bit when I asked them.

Don't work for morons

This seems like a simple task, but it is difficult to accomplish because of the number of morons out there. As the interviewee, you should try to look for signs that your interviewer is a moron. I would also check industry publications to see if the company you are interviewing with is newsworthy. Newsworthy does not mean that they are just in the newspaper or news. If they have to pay to get in the paper or news, that is not newsworthy. Newsworthy is when reporters pick up stories on the firm that show they are winning business, adding talent to their team, or adding other divisions by building them or purchasing them. I know that several of the folks I have recruited have checked on me and my firm to ensure they were not working with morons.

I have seen a few traits that definitely prove to me that someone is a moron. One is when people refer to the past as "the good ole days." They waste the present and the future, not by looking for new solutions to new problems but by trying to catalog a new problem as an old problem and using a solution from the past. You can predict the outcome of this strategy.

Another is taking credit for wins that their team or a team member has achieved. I call these folks "turf grabbers." They have never had an original thought themselves, but steal them from others. They generally work in mediocre firms or in divisions run by other morons.

Let's say that you have passed the first round of interviews and landed a job with a decent company and have a decent supervisor. Count yourself lucky. However, you need to be very careful. If you are good at what you do and there is mediocrity around you, moronity can nail you at any time. It is sort of like getting twitterpated in the Bambi movie. One day you are a normal, hardworking person and then, BAM! you are a moron. Watch for the signs. A list of characteristics follows later in this chapter.

In many organizations, moronity can become rampant, and most morons are on the lookout for fresh meat. The folks that used to work for them have quit, broken away from them somehow, or have been promoted into the "moron club." One telltale sign is that these folks come into work late and leave early. That doesn't necessarily mean that a person is a moron, but if you add not getting anything tangible done and blaming everyone else for problems, you probably have a moron. Oh, what a pity and a shame to see these death eaters suck some very great talent into the whirlpool of destruction.

Don't hire morons

It is a pity that it is so difficult, or impossible, to interview and screen for this negative trait. You can review a candidate's academic achievements, how the person reached for and accepted leadership positions, and then worked through professional life. Some recruiters think with their tests and their questions they can screen these folks out but, with the number of morons I see working, this is obviously not the case. Even after checking references, it is hard to uncover moronity. Previous supervisors are usually more than happy to send the moron to the competition. Many people think that by screening people by grades or achievement, you can screen out moronity.

You may be a moron

If you don't think you have worked *for* a moron, have worked *with* a moron, or have *had* a moron work for you, you may want to check in the mirror. There is always a moron around somewhere.

The following list of traits will help determine moronity. If you are not a moron, this will seem like a review of the first few chapters of this book.

You may be a moron...

- If you are taking advice from people who do not do what you want to do, you are a moron!
- If you don't have written goals, you could be a moron!
- If you are working for a moron, figure it out, but don't quit; you are a moron!
- If you actually have or have only thought about bringing a parent to an interview, you are definitely and completely a moron!

This is a true, funny, yet sad story. I was having a series of interviews for an internship. By the way, I am always amazed at how some candidates come off so brilliant and driven and how other candidates seem so mediocre and lazy.

Anyway, my team was having a series of interviews. They had the candidates sit in separate conference rooms while we moved to each interview. When we walked in, the candidates would step forward, shake our hand, and introduce themselves—if they were any good at interviewing. Like all salespersons, I am always being interviewed for an assignment either formally or informally so I take this interview process seriously. After completing several interviews, I walked into a conference room, expecting to see a single candidate in the room. When I saw a couple of people there, I excused myself, thinking I was in the wrong room. I ran around, looking for the assistant who had scheduled these interviews to make sure I was in the correct room. Once I confirmed that I was indeed in the right room, I walked back in, introduced myself, and shook hands with the candidate and his mom!

I wasn't ready for this! I had been on one side of an interview or another hundreds of times and had never heard or seen anything like this. The young man applying for the internship was obviously a mamma's boy! This woman was taking "soccer mom" to the extreme! I was stumped on how to proceed. I started the interview but was mystified as to why she was there. It seemed like the young man would have done a great job if she weren't there, and he was obviously *very* uncomfortable with her being there. She had obviously coached her son with his responses and questions, and she obviously had done her fashion homework (they both looked very professional). It was one of the better interviews that I had, but I couldn't figure out who would take the internship. If they both were hired, how should we pay them? Hmmmm!

I think I need to talk a bit about another issue besides just moronity in this chapter. It is a trait that attaches to a person that has turned or is turning into a moron. So, once this happens to you or you see it happening to others, do yourselves (or them) a favor and try to talk some sense into them.

Mediocrity

Don't be or become mediocre

I always love watching someone doing something that a mediocre person has said couldn't be done.

Mediocrity has to be the most tolerated and most damaging behavior in an organization. It is also the reason that organizations and people cannot effect positive momentum. Not only do these people slow themselves down, but they usually slow down the workings of the entire organization with their mediocre traits.

This is especially true when the head of the organization is mediocre. If you see that your organization is becoming mediocre, you can exert huge amounts of energy to change it, or leave before you become mediocre. There is no way to feel rewarded working with a bunch of mediocre duds. We read in the book of Revelations, "I know your doings; you are neither cold nor hot; I would that you were cold or hot! Accordingly, because you are lukewarm and neither hot nor cold, before long I will vomit you out of My mouth." Mediocrity is the same, and it should give everyone that same reaction.

This is a well-known issue in organizations; it seems that many business books and seminars espouse metrics for measuring an organization's mediocrity or show "new" ways for organizations or individuals to avoid mediocrity. There seems to be an unending need for these books and seminars. I have seen mediocre people read every one of these books, and then attend the seminars and continue to be mediocre. I guess since there are so many seminars and books on the subject, every once in a while, some mediocre person is saved.

My granddad had a saying: "If you have on white gloves and stick your hand in the mud, your gloves are going to get muddy. The mud will never get glovey."

Once mediocre people get into the organization, mediocrity becomes a cancer. The mediocre behavior spreads and will have to be cut out. Once people who are striving for excellence see their mediocre boss or colleague getting away with not being excellent, while getting the same pay and benefits as the people who strive for excellence in their work, they leave the firm to go to another firm where they can excel. These organizations will lose the people who are striving to be the best to other competing firms. As employees slide into mediocrity, it can slowly destroy the firm. Getting rid of mediocrity is easier to deal with early. Like a cancer, early detection and treatment can save the organization.

It is understandable for a mediocre manager to hire only mediocre staff; that way, the manager won't look mediocre. I know that non-mediocre folks try to hire people who are or can become better than they are. They are looking to build excellence and want to be pushed toward that goal for themselves, their partners, and their company.

Mediocrity breeds paranoia. If you see mediocrity or the telltale trait of paranoia, run away—

unless, of course, you are a paranoid, moronic, mediocre person yourself.

If you think you are a moron or turning into a moron, you can be saved

It is never too late to stop the spiral of mediocrity or moronity, but you have to work at it. If you start hurtling toward moronity, you will spiral faster and faster, out of control. You have to recognize that you have the traits, stop that momentum, and reverse all of those tendencies. This is particularly hard since being a moron is so easy. It is easy to blame others, not make your own decisions, and take credit for other people's successes.

TAKEAWAY: Don't be a moron. It's that simple. Life is tough, but it is even tougher if you surround yourself with morons or are a moron. "Good is the mortal enemy of Great"

CHAPTER 7—
HOW NOT TO GET A JOB

Do *not* do what I am about to describe.

At least once a week, people that I have never met with, heard of, or spoken to, send me their resumes. I keep the resumes in my in-box or carry them in my briefcase until people call to follow up. Amazingly, most never do. What should I do with these resumes? I used to use them for kindling; now, since I'm trying to be "green," I shred and recycle them.

I have never understood why people think that they can submit an application or resume to an unknown company or to an unknown person. How can people think that this unknown person would call *them* about their resume? The person sending the resume must take the initiative, and this is especially important if you are trying to land a sales job. If you can't sell yourself, how will you be able to sell a product?

Instead of hoping that you get a job by being lucky, take a "rifle" approach versus a "shotgun" approach by finding out where you want to begin and doing it on purpose. Luck is not a good strategy or business plan! Do yourself a huge favor: instead of wasting time randomly sending out resumes, spend your time doing research.

Go to the Internet—you know, the thing that Al Gore invented—and investigate the industry you want to work in. Read articles about the industry, and you will start to see the same firms mentioned. In most circumstances, the people quoted in those articles are the "movers and shakers" in that industry. Make a list of those people and continue researching them.

Now your work really starts. I call this part "triangulating relationships." The more you develop this skill, the more easily you will be able to first get into the industry you want and then land the job you want. This skill will work for you throughout your career—people who do it well usually do better with clients.

Triangulating relationships means finding some connection between you and the person you want to meet. The movers and shakers often speak at their industry meetings. You may want to join one of these organizations. Most of them allow discounted memberships for students or offer limited free memberships for students. While at these events, meet the person you want to send your resume to as well as other attendees; this will help you to decide if you want to work with these people.

While doing your homework, you may find ways of triangulating with people that aren't business related. You may find that you went to the same schools, have the same hobbies, or go to the same church or synagogue. If that is the case, again go to the places they frequent and introduce yourself.

You may be one of the lucky ones who went to a special school or had a lifetime friend that knows the very person you need to get to and can make the introduction for you. If this is not the case, the triangulating relationship process will be difficult and time consuming but ultimately rewarding. Begin this process as soon as you have selected an industry. You will not be able to start and finish this process the day before you start looking for a position. This process is time consuming.

A word of caution: if you have had someone help you get the internship, interview, or job, make sure that you do a terrific job. It isn't just your reputation that is on the line but also the reputation of the person who helped you.

Sending resumes to individuals at organizations where you want to work, without at least having a phone conversation with someone there, is a waste of time and energy. Your resume will end up in the shredder, or worse, in the human resources filing cabinet where they keep resumes they don't know what to do with. This may offend some of you, but smart candidates work hard to be hired and do their homework.

Here are some helpful suggestions:

- Research the companies in the industry, as well as the division in that firm that interests you the most.
- Once you have that information, research the people in that area, and schedule an informational interview with them.
- Do not assume that you can do this a few days before you graduate.
- Begin a dialogue with them as soon as possible so that they can coach you through your classes while you are still in school.
- Work with them to find an internship in that field.

Working in the real world is very different from reading about it or listening to someone who has no experience.

A student contacted me (through a friend of a friend), and she asked if she could take me to breakfast and ask me about my career. It took a few attempts to connect due to scheduling conflicts, but we finally got together. She was a sophomore in college and she was trying to decide which real estate classes would help her obtain and keep a real estate job. She had done a lot of research on my firm and on other firms as well. She had taken the time to research several professionals in the real estate business and wanted to get my perspective on her ability to work with them and their firms. She had checked with the other firms, found out if they offered internships, and wanted my opinion on which one she should pursue.

Because she was so prepared and inquisitive, I had no problem helping her with her class decisions and getting an internship. She has now graduated from college and is working in the real estate industry for one of my competitors. This is an example of the right actions to take.

In business, we often say, "The harder I work, the luckier I get." Some people will think this young woman was lucky, but doing her homework led her to a logical discussion about her classes and her future career.

On the flip side, a friend of a friend arranged a meeting for a young man who was about to graduate from college. Unlike the first example, this fellow was graduating in two weeks. Sadly, most of the meetings I have like this one do not turn out very well. Because of a relationship with the friend of a friend, I was ambushed into attending a meeting with a fellow who had not done any homework. He wanted me to explain my industry, my company, how it compared to its competitive group, and the industry in general. He should have known the answers to all these questions before our meeting. Coming to a meeting so unprepared is not a good way to impress anyone. In fact, it is rude. You will assume that the person is either lazy, has a sense of entitlement, is extremely naïve, or is arrogant. These types of meetings never go well.

If approached in the manner that I was by these college students, most executives would give the same instructions.

One other thing to review here is about your interview. It seems like a lot of people get very nervous or scared about this process. Don't. If you have done your homework about the firm and the interviewer(s), then you will do fine. You should never come off cocky, but you should have the attitude that you are interviewing them as much as they are interviewing you. The people you are being interviewed by will be impressed you have done your homework. Ask them questions like, what will my day look like? What will my tasks be? To whom will I report? How will I advance and who decides on my advancement? Are there any skills I need to focus on?

When you do this properly, you will have impressed them and it should put you in a better position to get that job.

TAKEAWAY: Keep your resume out of the shredder or the HR filing cabinet! Do not send your resume out blindly, and keep your reputation intact by following the advice described here. Make sure you are ready for the interview. Do your homework.

CHAPTER 8—HOW TO LOSE A JOB QUICKLY

I can summarize this chapter in one sentence: "If you do a great job where you are, you will always have a great job." It is really that easy *and* that hard.

I see many people who just try to get by and never seem to understand why they are the first ones to be laid off or why they don't get promoted. They complain that other people in the organization are doing something "special" with their superior. That is ridiculous.

The people who are succeeding are the ones taking the initiative, putting in the time, and trying to make the company better. Merely coming into the office and spending the minimum amount of time doing only what others ask of you is not the way to longevity or promotions. Why would anyone be advanced just doing the minimum? That only happens in mediocre companies.

My team just fired a young man who didn't figure this out. This person had gone to a fine college and received a useful degree. He interviewed well and came into the job expecting to learn and grow quickly. He did reasonably decent work at first and he would have made a good employee except for a few issues.

First, he wasn't very fast at his job, and even though he received plenty of training and support, he wasn't getting any faster. Second, after a month or so, he started going home at five o'clock every afternoon. If you think it was a bit rough for us to fire him over this, the service industry may not be for you. The industry is demanding, and it is a lifestyle choice, a fact that we explained to him many times. In our office, everyone works until of the managing directors leave. This allows the junior members of the firm to complete tasks demanded by clients.

Because he was doing well in other ways, some partners spent time trying to figure out how they could help him improve his work. We gently prodded him about why he went home every day at five. He confided in one of the partners that if he got his work done quickly, he was given more work. He also said that he left early because he had gotten a puppy and he wanted to go home and play with it. Neither excuse endeared him to the partners!

We gave him a week to improve his speed and told that him that he would be fired if he left before everyone else. I guess he didn't believe us, because the next day he left at five. His personal items were in the lobby the next morning. Two days after this happened; his father called and thanked us. The father was a successful attorney and had warned his son not to act the way he did.

The story has a happy ending. Because we sent him on his way, the young man has started another job and is working out well there. He called and thanked us for the coaching, as it allowed him to get his priorities in order.

As discussed earlier, research the personality needed, the education required, and the time expectations for the jobs you are considering. Some jobs require eight hours of work per day; others will take up most of your time. It is critical to look in the mirror and make sure the same thing is looking out that is looking in. If you are honest with yourself you will choose the correct path; if not, you will be miserable.

TAKEAWAY: Doing the minimum is the fast track to unemployment. People who excel, over deliver, and outwork the competition get ahead in the business world.

Nothing is really work unless you would
rather be doing something else.
~James Matthew Barrie

The supreme accomplishment is to blur the
line between work and play.
~Arnold Toynbee

If a man love the labour of any trade apart
from any question of success or fame, the
gods have called him.
~Robert Louis Stevenson

Don't waste time learning the "tricks of the
trade." Instead, learn the trade.
~Attributed to James Charlton and H.
Jackson Brown, Jr.

Choose a job you love, and you will never
have to work a day in your life.
~Confucius

The difference between a job and a
career is the difference between forty and
sixty hours a week.
~Robert Frost

What is it that you like doing? If you don't
like it, get out of it, because you'll be
lousy at it.
~Lee Iacocca

CHAPTER 9—WORK UNTIL YOU'RE ONE HUNDRED (OR DIE AT YOUR DESK)

I spoke to a class of undergrads and MBA students the other day; and after my presentation, I asked them what their biggest concern was for life after they graduated. The majority said that their largest concern was not just getting a job but getting a "perfect" job. They spoke about the difficulty of deciding between the many paths and knowing which job would lead them to the outcome they desired. I suppose that everyone looking for a meaningful career would have that same concern. As you can imagine, that wasn't one of the questions I had prepared for. They had definitely stumped the speaker! After thinking about the question for a few moments, I told them this story.

My dad is in his eighties, and my father-in-law is in his seventies. Both men work hard at their professions and they are still enjoying their lives and their work. They both rise early and enjoy what they do.

Both my dad and my father-in-law have had several careers over their years, and they enjoyed some more than others. They have continued to be curious about life. Even though they worked at some jobs just to support their families, they had their eye on the far horizon. They were constantly seeking to add to their skills and leverage them into jobs that better used those skills. They constantly sought more challenging and enjoyable situations. They both started working for other people and then ended up launching their own companies. (Some people take this path and enjoy the challenges of having their own business, and some will choose to work for others' businesses. Either way, the key is to thoroughly enjoy what you do.)

As we live longer, we may be able to work productively when we are a hundred years old. You may not want to think about having to work for that long! The good news is that your first job won't be your last job, and although your first job is important, it is not as critical as you may think. Your first job should get you off to a good start. At my age, I could go back to a university and start over with another major, or I could add onto my degree, write a book, or do something completely different. Again, the key is to find something that you enjoy. It will be great to work at something you enjoy until you are a hundred, but it will be drudgery to work until you are a hundred and hate every day.

While you are thinking about what you want to do "when you grow up," there is a great difference between studying about the career you think would be great for you, learning the skills needed to do that job, and actually doing it. Think of it as if you were studying to be a pilot versus flying. You have to acquire the "book smarts" to pass the examination and receive your license, but these alone will not help you to get airborne. You have to get into the plane and learn how to fly!

Think of preparing to work in a medical professional versus the business of that profession. While you may think that the work will be challenging and rewarding, you still have to bill patients, deal with insurance claims, and work with governmental agencies that dictate your fees by paying only so much for each procedure. I know doctors who love their profession because they wish to help people get well but despise the business of being a doctor. Some despise it so much that they quit and use their skills in other areas. It is too bad that before they spent so much time, effort, and money preparing for what they thought would be their profession they did not investigate the business part.

The great thing about working for many years is that you can mess up a few times and still have time to find a career that you really enjoy.

A word of caution; while I really enjoy my career, I dislike certain tasks. I try to finish those nasty tasks the first thing in the morning so that I won't have to think about them all day (or all week). If you are spending more than a quarter of your time doing tasks that you do not enjoy, move on to a new field. You are probably miserable, and you will make everyone that you interact with miserable as well.

There is one very critical step that people should take in order to make sure they are on the right path. To decide if you like the profession, the business side of that profession, and the people in that profession, intern with a company. Once you decide that you would enjoy this profession, you should complete your studies. Figure out what you think you want to do, find people who do it, see what they did right or wrong to get there, and then go do it.

TAKEAWAY: Stay curious. Keep your eye on the horizon. If you don't *love* your first job, you have time to figure out what you would rather do. Interning before committing is extremely helpful.

Networking is an essential part
of building wealth.
~Armstrong Williams

The richest people in the world look for and
build networks, everyone else looks for work.
~Robert T. Kiyosaki, entrepreneur

It's the oldest, corniest piece of advice
in the world but it still works. The strongest
networks are built on friendship. Be a friend
not only to the people in your network but
to the people who matter the most to the
people in your network.
~Harvey Mackay, businessman and author

Network continually; 85 percent of all
jobs are filled through contacts and
personal references.
~Brian Tracy, author and
motivational speaker

Technology does not run an
enterprise, relationships do.
~Patricia Fripp, author and success coach

If you're not networking, you're not
working.
~Denis Waitley, author, psychologist, and
motivational speaker

CHAPTER 10—NETWORK BEFORE YOU NEED TO

Throughout my career, I have watched many people work diligently but without focus in their careers. They seem to get stuck on autopilot and eventually get comfortable in their situation. They usually develop an air of smugness that garners a sense of complacency. They know a few people around the office and go to a few of the company functions such as the annual Christmas party. They seem to feel good about their jobs and do not get to know any of their peers outside their firm. They mistakenly feel that there is no reason to do much networking because they do their job.

Then a catastrophe strikes: the company downsizes, there's a merger, or they are fired. They go into panic mode and try to start networking to find another job. Some will go to a "headhunter" or an employment agency. I'm not suggesting that using a headhunter isn't a good way to find a job, but if your industry is cutting back, it can be difficult for a recruiter to help you. Once your industry is in this predicament, it will be difficult for anyone to get work. You should already have been networking. I don't understand why some people behave this way.

A friend of mine, whom I met early in my career, worked for a large corporation. Toward the beginning of her career, she went to industry functions and got to know a few people outside her firm but never really kept in touch with any of them. She had many chances to assist the many industry organizations where she belonged. She was good at her job, and everyone in her firm thought she would work her way up the corporate ladder. As she attained new positions and responsibilities, she quit attending outside functions she was formerly involved with and focused only on internal functions.

Then her company was purchased, and she was laid off. She had some good references and friends who had also been laid off in the merger, but she didn't know anyone at the firms where she wanted to get hired. After a few months of job searching, she told me that she didn't understand why some people that she had worked with, who were not as good as she was at her job, were getting hired and she wasn't. She assumed that the only reason people got hired was because of job performance.

That was twenty years ago, and this woman has repeatedly been the victim of mergers and acquisitions in our industry. She never took the advice of her friends: network continually. It seemed like every few years she was looking for employment and wanting to meet with folks whom she hadn't spoken to since the last time she needed help finding a job. She wanted the names of companies, the names of the people that were hiring, and she asked for references. Sadly, no matter how much you may want to help, you end up dodging people like her.

Please listen to this. If not, you may need to re-read the moron chapter. Business is about using skills and getting your job done. You need to continually work on improving your skills so that you can perform your job as well or better than anyone at your firm. However, if no one outside your firm knows about your abilities, it can be difficult to convince a new employer that you are great at your profession if they don't know you, and they know you were laid off.

The ability to network is a crucial skill. The best reason to have this critical skill is it will allow you to continually have doors open for you. By networking inside and outside your industry, you will always know of career opportunities and advancement.

You will continually meet the peers that you will be working with during your career. Because you never know what might happen at your firm or in your industry, monitor what others in similar positions are doing. As time goes by, you will see that some of your peers decide to leave their business and you may have the opportunity to work at their firm. You may even learn ahead of time that they are leaving and, with their help, get their position before the competition does.

At networking functions, you get to know both your peers and their bosses. Be careful not to befriend someone just so you can meet his or her boss—this move is very transparent, and you can easily lose a friend.

Throughout your career, you will be promoted above some of your peers, stay at the same level as some, or be subordinate to some in title or responsibility. This is normal. It will allow you to know people up and down the corporate chain so that you can hire or be hired by someone you know.

A second reason to network is that it helps to ensure that you are being treated and paid properly. You will want to know that you are receiving a pay rate, including benefits and perks that are equal to those of your peers. You will also want to know what positions are available at other firms.

A third reason is integration. Integrators are born, not made. When you start out in your career, you will find that some people learn quickly and then will start to investigate and experiment trying to add to the efficiency of their system or help streamline their processes. Oftentimes, they succeed in finding a newer, faster, or more efficient way to do their job. These folks have a small group, including people inside and outside of their firm that they bounce ideas off. You may think that this is against some company's policies. It may be, but because it happens, you may want to seek out those who initiate these changes and include yourself. The changes I have seen show initiative of individuals or teams. When they are under stress of getting projects completed in a short time they will come up with ways to streamline the process or once the project is done they will get together and develop a better use of the software they have been using.

The fourth reason to network is to make certain that your current team or company appreciates you. Finding career opportunities is much easier when you have personal relationships with other professionals in your industry. Sometimes the folks who trained you and work with you don't appreciate your skills and abilities and may curtail your growth. When this happens, use your network to find another position or leverage your current situation into one with more responsibility and/or better pay. Strive to do so well in your current position that your boss is concerned about losing you.

We seldom network *outside* our profession, but if you will, there will be benefits you will learn.

One reason is to see what integrations other industries are using that might benefit your industry. Some industries lag behind others in technology and other systems, possibly because some of these firms and their leaders made their way and fortunes before the technology era. If these leaders want to attract a young talented work force, they will need to spend the money to use technology to make their firm more efficient. These firms usually morph into larger firms and will attract workers who understand the importance of technology. If the leaders of these firms do not change so they can attract these younger workers, their firms usually cease to compete and then will usually cease to exist.

Network with your peers outside your industry so that you don't miss out on a vocation that might better fit your personality. If you think that you have found your true calling through meeting someone and learning what the person does, remember that you have to find out what skills are necessary and what personality type is a good fit before you leave your current position. Remember, "The grass isn't always greener on the other side of the fence."

A friend of mine was active in our industry organizations. He started attending a mixed organization that included real estate professionals as well as mortgage brokers, investment bankers, and attorneys. He struck up a friendship with one of the investment bankers, and when the industry started to expand rapidly, he was hired at an investment bank rather than a real estate brokerage company. This type of change is rare, and if the broker hadn't been networking outside of his industry, he would never have had the opportunity to work on Wall Street.

When used properly and with the right attitude, these different networking groups will pay dividends throughout your career.

To summarize the benefits of networking:
• Network to open doors for career opportunities and advancement.

- You have to network inside your industry or risk having difficulty if there is any catastrophe that causes you to lose your job.
- You may find a small group that is making headway into new and challenging integrations in your industry.
- You will meet and get to know peers that you might work with for the rest of your career.
- You will know that your firm is treating you fairly (regarding compensation and responsibility) compared to your peers.
- You need to make and keep industry friends. Some may want to hire you or become your partner.
- You should find it challenging and interesting to network outside of your industry.
- You may find a best practice that allows you to move up in your company or provides a more efficient way to do your job.
- If you are in sales, you will get business for your firm by doing a great job of networking.
- You may find that you are more suited for the other profession, in terms of both skills and personality.
- There are times that even morons will do a good job of networking and get great positions.

TAKEAWAY: Always look to enhance your relationships within and outside of your industry. You never know whom you will meet, whom you might get to work with, or how you can learn something that increases your knowledge and skills.

Success is simply a matter of luck. Ask any failure.
~Earl Wilson

I don't know the key to success, but the key to failure is trying to please everybody.
~Bill Cosby

Try not to become a man of success, but rather try to become a man of value.
~Albert Einstein

As you climb the ladder of success, be sure it's leaning against the right building.
~Quoted in *P.S. I Love You*, compiled by H. Jackson Brown, Jr.

There is no point at which you can say, "Well, I'm successful now. I might as well take a nap."
~Carrie Fisher

Some people dream of success while others wake up and work hard at it.
~Unknown

Those who have succeeded at anything and don't mention luck are kidding themselves.
~Larry King

CHAPTER 11—DO WHAT UNSUCCESSFUL PEOPLE WON'T

That person is so lucky! It seems that they are always getting the best assignment, the best job, the best "whatever." Have you ever heard this? Of course you have. People who have decided that they don't want to be successful say it repeatedly. Why do I say that? Perhaps we should ask the people who say these things why they won't do what successful people will do. Why do they ignore someone else's hard work and their own inability to do what it takes?

Let's take a look at what professional athletes will do to be successful. You may look up to these people, and you probably know something of what it takes to achieve at their level. You may have tried out for a sports team of some kind and seen people who push to go to the next level become derisive if you do not push yourself as hard. I have known this same type of person and know how driven and passionate they are about their job. Interestingly, they don't usually think of it as a job, it is their passion. These athletes test the limits of their bodies over and over. They discipline themselves to get the most out of themselves. Some who are already great reinvent themselves so that they can become even better or more dominant. One person who comes to mind is Tiger Woods. Arguably one of the greatest golfers, he is also extremely disciplined in his practice and his focus on his sport. He completely changed his swing *after* he was the best in the world. That is amazing! Would you have the guts to remake yourself if you knew it *might* make you better at what you do?

In the business world, many people sit around watching other people perform, ooh and aah about their performance, but then whine when they won't discipline themselves in their job. If you put in the same time, effort, and discipline of high performers, you can stop whining and be success-ful. What's sad is that most of you won't do these things and someone who will do them will get to make the money and the position you wanted.

In my professional life, I am extremely disciplined and I am always looking to expand my knowledge and become more efficient. I think that the rea-son for my discipline and passion is my true love of my career. (I assume that Dirk Nowitzki, The MVP of the Dallas Mavericks is not as passionate about anything as much as he is about basketball and he possibly would not excel in anything like he has basketball.) There are many things I do not do well because I don't like doing them, and if they were my vocation, I would be a mediocre performer.

The first thing to do that unsuccessful people won't is to find what you are really passionate about. Just because you may be passionate at golf, you may not be able to play at the level to get paid. That is a pity, but you may be a great caddie or have the ability to work in the "golf" industry doing other things.

It seems the media loves kicking people when they are down. The media focuses on athletes who have taken or presumed to have taken performance-enhancing drugs. While I really don't care what these people do since I see them only as entertainment, they do have their rules and these people are cheating. Be the best you can without cheating. I think I would have a huge internal issue "succeeding" if I cheated. I think there have been athletes that have returned medals and other awards because their conscience bothered them.

The list below includes guidelines that successful people will follow and unsuccessful people won't. I know that some successful people have talents in these areas and take them for granted while others do not have that innate ability and have to work hard to have these skills. It is only a partial list, but a good start.

Learn to persuade

Whether we like it or not, this is the one skill we need in both the business world and in all aspects of life. From the day we are born, we learn how to persuade others. This starts out as crying and screaming for food, attention, and sleep, whatever. As we mature, we learn new and more acceptable ways of persuasion instead of crying and screaming for everything. Some have learned this skill while others have not.

I know many successful people who aren't the hardest working, the most creative, or the most impressive, but they have the ability to persuade. You can have brilliant ideas, but if you can't get them across persuasively, your ideas won't get you anywhere.

The faster you learn this life lesson, the faster you will be able to succeed in your life. If you cannot persuade, you may never get the job, the spouse, the raise, or whatever you are trying to get or achieve. This is not just learning how to communicate verbally or in written format but using those skills to persuade people to have them do the things you are wanting to accomplish. You would think that good ideas would be easy to sell in the business world or in your personal life. Not so.

The art of persuasion can seem natural for some people and very difficult for others. I believe that is true up to a point, but like writing and speaking, developing and training those skills until you become an expert will allow you to look like you are a natural at all three of these skills when, in fact, you have had to focus on and work hard at becoming "a natural" at them.

Over the past decade, I have gone to a "presentation coach," Gary Hankins, author of *The Power of the Pitch: Transform Yourself into a Persuasive Presenter and Win More Business*. This is not a speech class, but it teaches you to present and persuade. He shares tips and advice on many things, including how to dress, but more importantly, he explains the process of presenting and persuading.

TAKEAWAY: You need to become a master at persuasion in order to succeed in all aspects of your life. Learn to speak and write well, and then find a coach that will teach you how to persuade.

Learn everything you can

A fellow was riding on an airplane and noticed that his row mate was reading a large, hardback book about a famous historical figure. He noticed the price of the book, around $75. He blurted out that it was ridiculous to spend so much money on that book. The man looked up slowly, and said, "You know, it does seem expensive at first, but if by reading this book, I can learn what this man did during his life and use just a small portion of that in mine, the price is extremely cheap."

TAKEWAY: Be a student of life. Stay curious about everything.

Show up

I was a teenager at one time and never really wanted to do anything but sleep. My kids now always want to stay up most of the night and then can't get up the next morning. Now, that isn't that big of a deal in the summer, but it becomes one true "pain in the ass" during school. My wife and I seem to be always trying to get these people out of the house on time for school. It is definitely a life lesson. Here is another statistic. People who show up for work actually do better at that job than people who don't. You can assume 1,000 percent more successful if you need the percentage.

Are you one of those folks who barely make it to work on time, who are always a little late for meetings? This signals to the people who got there on time that their time is not as valuable as yours. How arrogant! This is truly a pet peeve for most executives that I know. Executives run to several meetings each day, and backing up their schedules because you were late will not serve you well. Eventually, you will not be attending the meetings at all. I know this seems old-fashioned; but when you are my age, you will be the same "old-fashioned" that I am now, because I used to think what you do about my "old-fashioned" bosses.

I was once in New York for a series of meetings with my colleagues, and we were seeing an important client. We had invited our CEO to the meeting and set the meeting up with the client's CEO (we will call him Mr. Big). We did this because our CEO was in the city on other business. Everything was going fine. We all arrived early, because after September 11, 2001, the security in New York office buildings is as daunting as any airport. We received our name tags from the guard, and we were escorted to the office.

While we were sitting and waiting on our time to meet, our CEO got a call and was still talking when Mr. Big's assistant came out to receive us into his conference room. We walked in, except our CEO, and were asked if we needed anything to drink. Once the assistant had delivered the drinks, Mr. Big entered the conference room.

Because we knew his time was valuable, we tried to start the meeting while we were waiting on our CEO. Mr. Big wouldn't allow us to begin until our CEO was present. I felt like we were at an expensive restaurant where we could not be seated until everyone was there. We sat and sat and sat. It seemed much longer than it probably was since we were all just looking around at each other. Mr. Big kept his cool and waited. Finally, after ten very long minutes, our CEO popped into the conference room with Mr. Big's assistant. Our CEO started by excusing himself by saying he had been on the phone and said the conversation he was having was about a "very big deal." I sure wish he hadn't said that in that way!

Mr. Big quietly and in a very dignified tone told my CEO that he had rudely detained not only him but all of his own colleagues that he was with and that *he* and his company were "a big deal." He let that sink in for a minute and proceeded to ask us to leave and never bother coming back to see him again. He then rang for his assistant, who ushered us out of the building. His company would still do business with ours but we never enjoyed the same relationship that we had before that meeting.

You may think that Mr. Big had too big an ego or that he overreacted. This is probably because you have never worked at this level. This is only one example of this and I would rather have someone tell me this to my face than to not hire me or fire me because of this. Most people find out the hard way how truly competitive our marketplace is and how easy it is to lose an account.

TAKEAWAY: Always show up, on time or early. You never know what can come up to detain you. Make being on time a habit!

Communication

Learn to do this and do it often!

There are so many problems that should have never occurred because of the lack of this critical skill. These will include all areas of life: relationships with friends, your girlfriend or boyfriend, your spouse, your boss, etc. These relationships can prosper or be destroyed, depending on communication.

This is not the same skill as persuasion. You will need this seemingly simple skill to carry on a conversation with others. Many people do not listen to what other people are saying and will rudely butt in or jump in before or right after the other person has quit speaking. This shows that they have not listened to the person and considered his or her point of view—only that you are only trying to make your own point. After a few conversations and meetings like these, people will tire of this and will try to stay away from you. It is hard to win business when clients don't want to talk with you.

TAKEAWAY: Learn to communicate so that people feel you have considered their thoughts and concerns. You will undoubtedly get more business, and people will like having you around as well.

Invest in yourself

Believe it or not, you will start making money someday. Hopefully, more money than you are spending. It seems like it will never be enough. When that happens, many people will try to get you to invest in one investment or another. Generally, what happens is that someone will tell you about the latest new deal to get into. They will tell you that there is no way you can lose. DO NOT BELIEVE THEM! They are trying to get your money. When an investment seems too good to be true, it is. Sadly, no one seems to be able to escape this rite of passage. I don't think I have ever met anyone who hasn't invested money badly. Instead of giving your money away, invest your money in yourself. This investment can take many forms. If you are working at a profession that has different accreditations, work on getting those so that your skills are up to date and the value of your time and skills continues to grow. If you aren't passionate about the career you have chosen, seek one that will allow you to be passionate, so you can enjoy your work. Take classes you need to get that next promotion or the next career started.

I started my career at a public accounting firm—back then, the firm I worked at was one of what we called the "Big 8." I had a prestigious job and career, but it was very demanding. I was in the tax department of the firm and found it to be very interesting. I was happy to continue to learn about the tax code and accounting.

I had friends that I worked with that wanted more from their degree and experience. I knew several people who went to law school at night and on weekends so that they could leverage their accounting and tax knowledge into the legal profession. They did this to continue to make their services more valuable. They invested time early in their career, so they could make more money (or work less for the same amount of money).

Some other professionals at the firm thought that the sacrifice of their free time was too much to ask of them. That wasn't a big deal until the people who didn't want to improve their skills, and therefore increase the value of their services, started complaining that they weren't paid as well as those who had put in additional time. You would think that folks who specialize in numbers would understand that you can charge more for greater expertise, and therefore people with those additional skills should be paid for that enhanced intelligence instead of just the amount of time they have worked for the firm.

TAKEAWAY: Invest in yourself. It is the best way to continue growth in your profession or your next career.

CHAPTER 12—OTHER THOUGHTS AND OPINIONS

This chapter is going to be different in that there will be some lessons I learned in life that will be good for you to know as well. I learned these the hard way—as I normally learn every lesson. I hope you will read through these lessons and learn them without the lumps I received.

All leverage or no leverage

Debt, n. An ingenious substitute for the chain and whip of the slavedriver. ~Ambrose Bierce, The Devil's Dictionary, 1911

Another lesson that I have learned in the past five decades is that there is no risk if you have 100 percent leverage (or debt) or 0 percent leverage. With 100 percent leverage, you shouldn't be tempted to continue fighting the creditors to protect any equity since there is none. If you have 100 percent equity, the investment could deflate in value, but you can hold the asset through a downturn without worrying about someone taking any remaining equity.

Ninety-day rule

Buy what thou hast no Need of and ere long thou shalt sell thy Necessaries. ~Benjamin Franklin

Here is an important way to learn to save your money; I call it the ninety-day rule. I learned this rule from my granddad. He was a product of the Great Depression and his values were quite a lot different from most folks' values these days. This will probably shock most of you, but he actually never had a credit card and never borrowed money for anything in his life. One of the ways he did this was to use the ninety-day rule. When he wanted to buy something, he would get a picture of it or write it down, put it in his wallet, and keep it with him for ninety days. If, after the ninety-day period, he still wanted to buy it, he would pay cash for it if the purchase didn't use money saved for family necessities.

Trying to instill this discipline in this spendthrift culture will be very difficult but will yield you a stress-free life. You will find that usually once the ninety-day period is over, you will either not want the item you couldn't live without or, you will have another item or two that you want even more. Usually, I never purchased a single item that I "had to have" once I applied the ninety-day rule. Now I am able to buy most anything I like, because I have finally learned to live without credit and have paid off all of that debt. I can't imagine having the additional stress of credit issues on top of the stress that stays with us just living these days.

The sacrifices you make early in your life will set you up for later in life. You won't have the cutest house or the coolest cars or gadgets, but you will have savings.

Save your money

He who does not economize will have to agonize. ~Confucius

Now I know you know this. It's kind of stupid to even have to put this into writing, but you can't fix stupid! I think the best way to do this is not to think about it, just do it! Take 10 percent of your gross earnings and put it in savings. Not 10 percent of your net earnings, but ten percent of the gross. This money needs to be put away so that you can't easily pull it out and spend it. Use the tax savings of an IRA program as much as possible, and max out your contributions every year. If possible, participate in your company's 401(k) program, especially if your company matches the funds you put in. Again, the best way to do this is to do it! When you can, make this on top of the 10 percent you are supposed to be already saving.

If you think you have many expenses now, and are fairly young (in your twenties, perhaps), just wait until you get a look at the list of things you will need to save for. You will have to save for all kinds of major life events: getting married, a house, furniture, children, your children's college tuition, cars, the children's marriages, vacations, and retirement. That is a lot of saving. Get accustomed to saving, and get good at it. All of the wealthier people I know save money even though they don't have to. It is part of their life-style.

Most people live from paycheck to paycheck, even people that seem to be very well off. I know one couple that seemed to be doing well financially. They had a large, beautiful house, brand-new expensive cars, and a jet. They jetted off to vacations around the world. They seemed to be all set until there was a small downturn in the economy. Because they were so leveraged professionally and personally, they lost all of the assets they thought were so important. Mistakenly, people think others are successful because they have fine automobiles and homes and they vacation in the finest places in the world. However, these folks can become destitute if something goes wrong in their business or if their family experiences some large, sudden expense. Know that these expenses will probably occur, or that a downturn will happen, and plan for these events.

Some of you will fall into the trap of high credit and blame everyone but yourself on always being behind and never having any money. There is a saying, "We work our fannies off to buy things to impress people we don't even like." Another saying I have heard says, "Live like the gentiles won't until you can live like the gentiles can't." This may be sensitive to some of you, but it shouldn't be. A lot of cultures save their money and live simply until they have the money they need to pay for the life-style they want—instead of spending themselves into near or actual poverty.

As I have stated earlier, I am not a student of statistics nor do I study things as simple as money matters. I just know from being around people that a lot of marriages, family relationships, worry, and heartache are because of money issues. Please save and use your money wisely so that you can avoid these issues. It really isn't that difficult. Live below your means instead of "keeping up with the Joneses" and trying to impress people you don't even like.

Don't overstay your welcome

Learn all you can and move on.

Your first job should last the longest since you really don't know anything when you get out of school except how to sit for long times in a chair and listen to long-winded folks. Be careful; some people that just got out of college tend to think they know everything. When I was just out of school, I thought the same since I had just spent the previous sixteen years learning. Once I figured out how little I knew, I actually started learning what I needed to know to do the job and career I selected. Make sure you learn everything you can at each job and from each person you meet. You will find that certain individuals are equally successful but approach their jobs differently. Usually this is for the simple reason that they have become successful even though their skills and personalities are radically different. Find a mentor who fits your skills and personality—you can learn from that person much quicker than trying to force your personality to match a profession.

As you have different positions throughout your career, you will continually add to your existing skills. If you feel that you have learned everything from an organization and the people you are working with, and your superior does not move you into a position that challenges you, it is time to move on. I will ask that you really take some time to look in the mirror and make certain you aren't kidding yourself. If you remember the chapter on networking, you will remember that you will be interacting with these people after you leave the company, so make sure that you leave for the right reasons.

As you continue to grow into different positions throughout your career, you will not need as much time to learn those new skills you need, since you will be continually augmenting skills you have already developed. Again, always use the filter of making sure you aren't kidding yourself and that the current organization and the people you work with would not agree to move you into a position that both challenges you and allows you to grow your skills. If you are certain this won't happen, then move on!

At some point, you will know that you are at the job in your career where you can truly excel. Once you have arrived at that place, make certain the organization hires people with strong values, skills, and ethics. Stay with them and help them grow the organization.

My career is a lot like this chapter. However, I really didn't have a strategy to move each time I thought I had learned all of the skills I could from the organization and their people. I usually just got bored. Reflecting back on all of the different firms I have had the pleasure of working with, it allowed me to meet many great people that I otherwise wouldn't have known well or at all. If I had known about this, I would have moved to different firms on purpose.

Do it on purpose!

"This is the true joy in life, the being used for a purpose recognized by yourself as a mighty one; the being thoroughly worn out before you are thrown on the scrap heap; the being a force of nature instead of a feverish selfish little clod of ailments and grievances complaining that the world will not devote itself to making you happy."
~George Bernard Shaw

While people seem to think they are doing this, I know from listening and watching different people and organizations that it is really an exception, not the rule. I think we all try to, but we get sidetracked or lack the discipline to finish. Your life will be judged by what you finish, not by your good intentions or the projects you start.

Getting it done sounds very simple but is actually very difficult. Set goals—give them a lot of introspection and thought. Ascertain your skills and your level of discipline to make sure that you can finish what you start. Once you have figured out what you want to accomplish, make sure that you have the time and resources to complete the goal. If it is a complicated task with many steps, break it down into small, achievable steps so that you can see progress being made.

Once you have your goal in mind and you have mapped out the process, do it!

Working hard will make you successful

The title of this chapter may confuse people who know me and have watched me throughout my career. As you know, I really enjoy what I do and continually tell everyone that I get to do my job for eight hours a day, and then get to work at my hobby another eight. My job and my hobby just so happen to be the same thing.

When I started working at the accounting firm, they required everyone to fill out a time sheet every day, so they could bill clients for time you worked on their behalf. This timekeeping irritated everyone there. They had to account for every thirty minutes of their time on a timesheet that had to add up to at least eight hours a day. At the beginning, this was difficult, because you didn't know exactly how long you took to go get a drink, to go to the bathroom, to chat with your friends, or to cruise by that good-looking associate who wasn't actually on the way to the bathroom. Additionally, other associates were "going to the bathroom" and coming by for chats. Or if you were one of the good-looking associates, you had to make certain you were presentable at all times. You finally figured out that if you wanted to put in the correct hours for the client and didn't want to spend a couple of extra hours at the office, you learned to focus your time and energy (and you asked the good-looking associate out for a cocktail and dinner). It was more productive for both work and play.

"The harder I work, the luckier I get" is an adage I would like to append by adding "smarter." It should state, "The harder I work smarter, the luckier I get." Obviously, this isn't quite as catchy, but it is definitely of more use to you.

Oppurnockity only tunes once

Jumping at several small opportunities may get us there more quickly than waiting for one big one to come along. ~Hugh Allen

A fable I heard quite awhile ago has stuck with me all of these years. It is a bit corny, like most fables, but like most fables, it has a great moral message.

There was a fellow named Vlatamere who owned an expensive, antique violin that had been handed down through his family for centuries. His family had always been comprised of master musicians. The violin was a work of art, and Vlatamere could play that violin as well as anyone in the world. He always searched for the finest accessories that he could afford to go with this fabulous violin. He had purchased a special case, a special bow, and, of course, the finest strings he could afford. The one issue with the violin was that it was difficult to tune. Because he was a master musician, he was very good at tuning the violin but wanted to find someone who could tune it more accurately. Obviously, the more accurately the violin was tuned, the better the music would sound.

One afternoon, a close friend of Vlatamere came running into his studio, exclaiming that he had heard there was a master musician who specialized in tuning instruments for other master musicians, and that his specialty was antique violins. Vlatamere was incredibly excited. Vlatamere asked his friend for this person's name and where he could be found. His friend told him the violin tuner was named Oppurnockity, and he lived in a cottage high in the mountains. When Vlatamere learned where the man lived, he was disappointed because it was a five-day hike into the mountains. But because he thought he had finally found this tuner, he decided to take the time and trouble to go see Oppurnockity and get his violin tuned.

The very next day, Vlatamere started the trek. He put his violin in its special case and headed into the mountains. He was so excited that he almost ran the whole way.

Once he got to the Oppurnockity's studio, he negotiated and paid for the tuning. Vlatamere watched as his violin was finally tuned to perfection. He held the violin and then played for a few minutes and could not believe how beautiful it sounded. He thanked Oppurnockity and raced home to perform for his family, and everyone was amazed how the violin sounded.

Like any stringed instrument, the violin eventually became out of tune. Vlatamere knew where to have the violin tuned, so he went back to Oppurnockity's studio. Oppurnockity opened the door and Vlatamere asked him to tune his violin once again. Oppurnockity shook his head and stated, "Oppurnockity only tunes once!"

I warned you about the corniness of the story! It presents a point that needs to be driven home. Take advantage of the opportunities that come your way. There is nothing as disgusting or boring than people who Wouda, Couda, Shouda.

Don't work with people who have more problems than you do

I know God will not give me anything I can't handle. I just wish that He didn't trust me so much. ~Mother Teresa

Wow, this can be incredibly difficult to do, especially if you have many problems. The issue with this situation is that the amount of time and energy needed while you are at work is usually very high and having a lot of personal issues can either take away from the work at hand or drain you emotionally so much that you either start making mistakes or, causing issues at work. When you have a boss, co-worker, or employee with personal issues, it is difficult to not become involved in them. Sadly, there are people around that I call "walking victims." These people always seem to have terrible issues in their lives. Their emotions can be draining for others around them and cause others to make mistakes at work.

I employed a person who had marital issues, then divorce issues, then getting married issues, then marital issues, then divorce issues. You get the drift! Along with these came the kid issues and then the finance issues and then more kid issues and more finance issues, then single parent issues and then more kid issues. No wonder this person was barely able to perform at work. These folks often end up getting fired, which worsens their "walking victim" scenario. Just think, now they can add getting fired, looking for a job, getting a job, getting fired, looking for a job.

Getting swept up in their problems will not help your career. Duh!

I have also had partners who had bad luck with their finances, spouses, children, and families. It takes time to reassess their situation and get back up on their feet, and usually their personal matters are fleshed out quickly. However, at times, they can spiral out of control, leaving you with a partner who cannot perform or is so frayed emotionally that he or she can devastate the environment at the office. If the person's role is that of an executive, it is difficult for junior partners and staff to ignore the emotional roller coaster. It can cause some of your talented partners and staff to leave for a less-turbulent environment.

Although I strive to keep away from these predicaments, you can see that I have experienced both staff and partner problems and probably always will. We are all humans, and we work with humans. When you recognize the situation, rectify it as quickly as possible. Sit down with the person having the issue and explain what damage he or she is causing at work and what you are prepared to do about it if this behavior does not change. You need to be willing to either let these folks go, or find another opportunity. Sadly, I have rarely seen one of these people come out of one of these downward spirals without help. Be careful in these situations, as it is better at times to allow the HR department to get involved if you feel you have done what you need to do. It is hard for me to take it to that level since they will have to document the situation.

CHAPTER 13—GO GET 'EM

I hope you have enjoyed learning some new strategies for your career. I wish you great luck in your future. These lessons I have presented won't guarantee your success, but they will improve your chances.

Whether you are just starting to move from high school to college or you are contemplating another degree or an advanced degree, think about what you want to accomplish. We discussed how to go about getting the correct advice and from whom, and we discussed success and education as well.

Once you have started working, the remaining chapters are more relevant. Things like making sure you know yourself with all of your strengths and weaknesses are crucial so that you select the correct career. Having written goals will help guide you through your life and career. Staying away from mediocrity and morons, knowing how to network better, triangulating your relationships, sending in resumes properly, having fun working and doing what unsuccessful people won't will get you where most only hope they will be!